W9-BWI-220

A+ books

Earth Matters

SUN POWER

A Book about Renewable Energy

by Esther Porter

Content Consultant:
Tom Fitz, PhD
Associate Professor of Geoscience
Northland College
Ashland, Wisconsin

CAPSTONE PRESS
a capstone imprint

Energy is all around us. It runs our cars and turns on our lights. It heats and cools our homes. We use energy to call our friends and to build our cities.

But where does energy come from?

2

Energy comes from natural resources. Energy is either renewable or nonrenewable. Renewable energy can be replaced. It does not run out.

Fossil fuels have given us energy for many years. But they are not perfect. **They are nonrenewable.**

Deep underground, heat, pressure, and time turn fossils into fuel. Coal, natural gas, and oil are fossil fuels. This kind of energy takes a long time to form, and we use it up quickly. **Using fossil fuels creates harmful pollution.**

We are lucky to have renewable sources of energy too. Much of our renewable energy is solar energy. It comes from the sun. **As long as the sun shines, we will have energy.**

The sun has been shining for billions
of years. Sunlight travels 186,000 miles
(300,000 kilometers) per second.
It takes eight minutes to reach Earth.
That is some amazing energy!

10

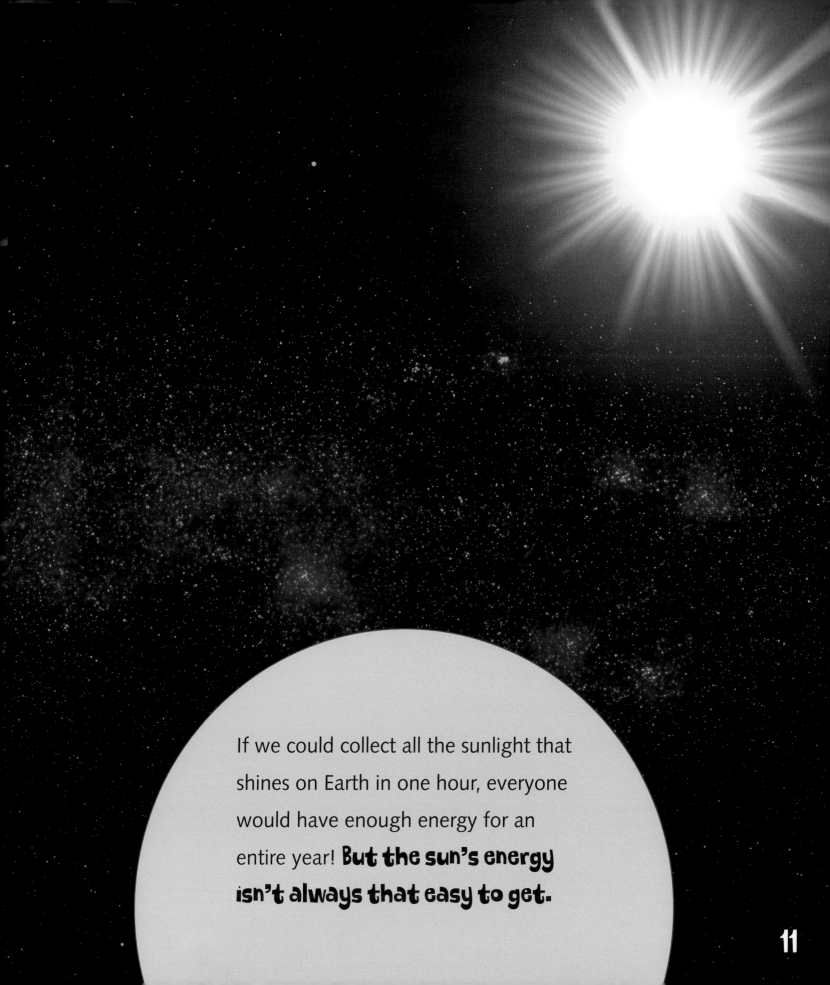

If we could collect all the sunlight that shines on Earth in one hour, everyone would have enough energy for an entire year! **But the sun's energy isn't always that easy to get.**

To use the sun's energy,
first you have to catch it. One way
is to gather sunlight with special
panels. Solar panels soak up sunlight
and change it into electricity.

Shiny mirrors also help collect the sun's rays. A field of mirrors reflects lots of sunlight to one spot for collection. **The sun plays a part in other kinds of renewable energy too.**

As the sun heats up Earth's atmosphere, it stirs up the clouds in the sky. The moving air can be used to provide power.

Wind is a renewable energy source collected with turbines. A turbine looks a lot like a fan. **It catches the wind with its large blades to create electricity.**

Where else do we
find renewable energy?
Water! This renewable energy is called
hydropower. It comes from the movement of water.
Dams and waterfalls catch a river's energy.

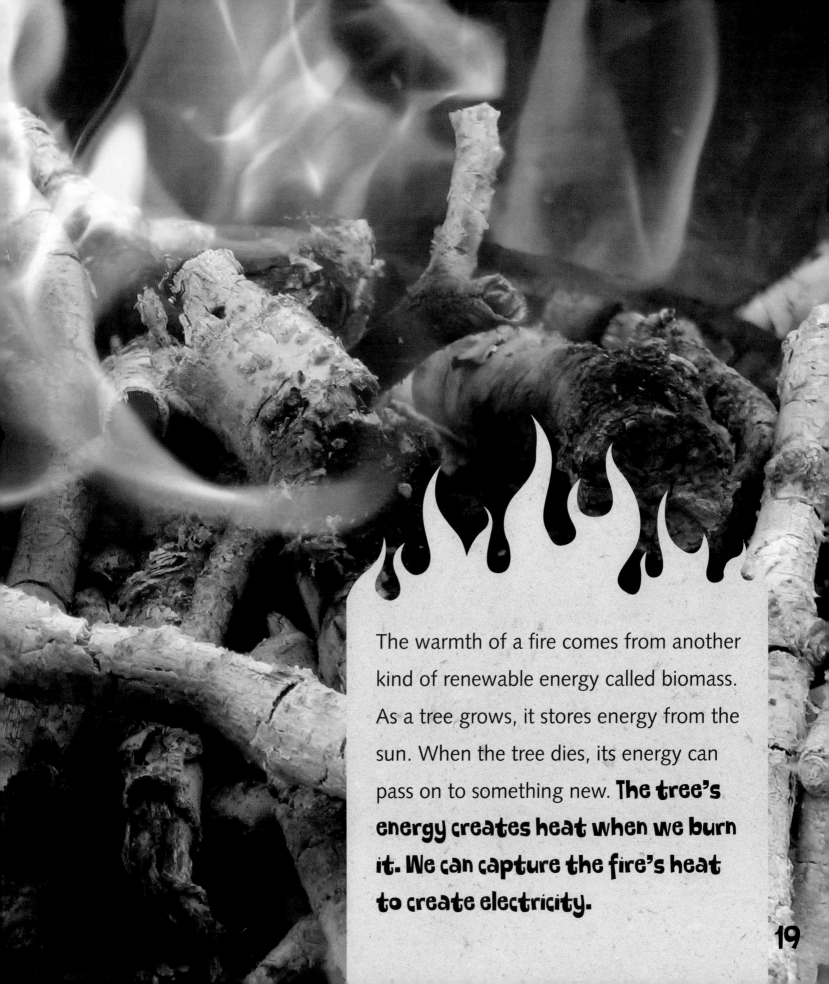

The warmth of a fire comes from another kind of renewable energy called biomass. As a tree grows, it stores energy from the sun. When the tree dies, its energy can pass on to something new. **The tree's energy creates heat when we burn it. We can capture the fire's heat to create electricity.**

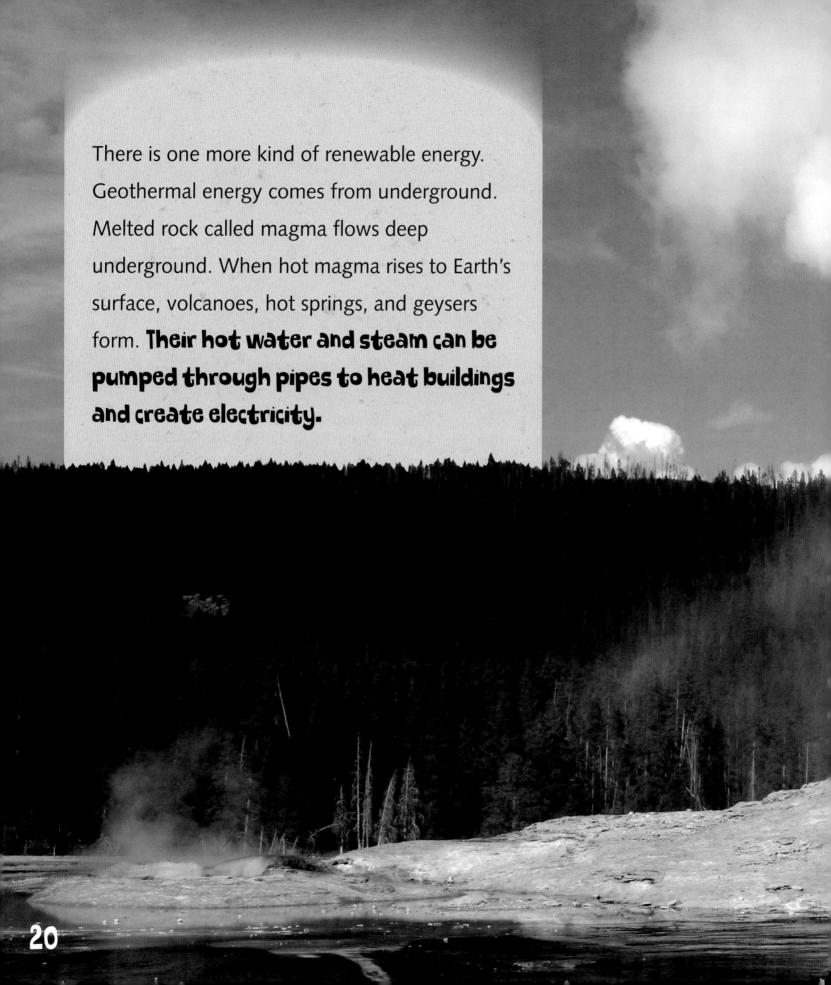

There is one more kind of renewable energy. Geothermal energy comes from underground. Melted rock called magma flows deep underground. When hot magma rises to Earth's surface, volcanoes, hot springs, and geysers form. **Their hot water and steam can be pumped through pipes to heat buildings and create electricity.**

21

These five types of
renewable energy work together in
one big cycle. The sun's heat moves through
air, water, plants, rock, and even through us.
**Can you guess why renewable
energy is important?**

The more renewable energy we use, the less nonrenewable energy we need. Our planet has always been able to renew itself naturally. **If we watch carefully, Earth can show us better ways to catch and use its energy.**

Your mind is the most important resource. By learning more about your world, you can make it a better place. **What do you think would be a good way to harness renewable energy?**

Make a Mini Wind Turbine!

Want to see how a wind turbine works? Make a pinwheel! Like wind turbines, pinwheels turn when air blows past them. Here's how to make your own:

You will need:

paper

pencil with an eraser on the end

crayons, markers, or colored pencils

scissors

pushpin

Instructions:

1. Use the pencil to trace the pattern shown on page 29 onto a piece of paper.

2. Color the square however you like.

3. Use the scissors to cut out the square.

4. Cut the four dashed lines. Do not cut all the way to the center!

5. Punch holes in the small circles with the pushpin.

6. Curl up the corners of the squares so the corner holes line up with the center hole.

7. Push the pushpin through all holes and into the side of the eraser.

8. Hold the pencil and blow straight into the center of your pinwheel.

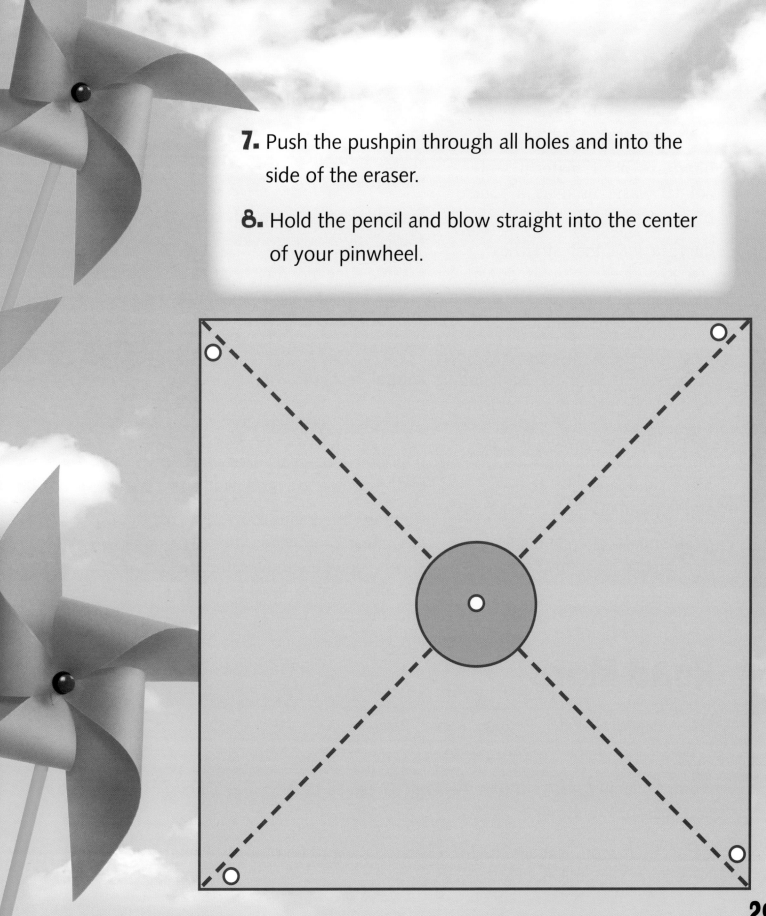

Glossary

atmosphere—the layer of gases that surrounds Earth

biomass—plant material and animal waste used as a source of fuel

dam—a wall that stretches across a river; it slows down the rushing water and raises the water level behind it

electricity—a form of energy that can be used to make light and heat or to make machines work

fossil fuel—a natural fuel formed from the remains of plants and animals; coal, oil, and natural gas are fossil fuels

geothermal—energy made from the intense heat inside Earth

geyser—an underground spring that shoots hot water and steam through a hole in the ground

hydropower—a form of energy caused by flowing water

magma—melted rock that is found beneath Earth's surface; after magma breaks through the surface, it is called lava

natural resource—something in nature that people use, such as coal, trees, and oil

pollution—materials that hurt Earth's water, air, and land

turbine—an engine powered by gas, steam, or wind; the gas, steam, or wind moves through the blades of a fanlike device and makes it turn

Read More

Fix, Alexandra. *Water.* Reduce, Reuse, Recycle. Chicago: Heinemann Library, 2008.

Hord, Colleen. *Clean and Green Energy.* Green Earth Discovery Library. Vero Beach, Fla.: Rourke, 2011.

Ramade-Masson, Isabelle. *Earth's Energy.* Taking Action for My Planet. New York: Windmill Books, 2010.

Internet Sites

FactHound offers a safe, fun way to find Internet sites related to this book. All of the sites on FactHound have been researched by our staff.

Here's all you do:

Visit *www.facthound.com*

Type in this code: 9781620650462

Check out projects, games and lots more at
www.capstonekids.com

Index

A+ Books are published by Capstone Press,
1710 Roe Crest Drive, North Mankato, Minnesota 56003
www.capstonepub.com

Library of Congress Cataloging-in-Publication Data
Porter, Esther.
Sun Power: A Book about Renewable Energy / by Esther Porter.
p. cm.—(A+ Books. Earth Matters)
Includes bibliographical references and index.
Summary: "Simple text and color photographs provide an introduction to renewable
energy"—Provided by publisher.
ISBN 978-1-62065-046-2 (library binding)
ISBN 978-1-62065-739-3 (paperback)
ISBN 978-1-4765-1092-7 (eBook PDF)
1. Solar energy—Juvenile literature. 2. Renewable natural resources—Juvenile literature. I. Title.
TJ810.3.P67 2013
621.042—dc23   2012023417

Editorial Credits
Jeni Wittrock, editor; Bobbie Nuytten, designer; Svetlana Zhurkin, media researcher;
Jennifer Walker, production specialist

Photo Credits
Corbis: Simon Jarratt, 26–27; Shutterstock: akiyoko, 6–7, Alex Staroseltsev, 1 (top), Bartosz Wardzinski, 20–21,
c. (cardboard texture), cover (top), Colin Stitt, 16–17, fotohunter, cover (left), Gabrielle Hovey, 18–19, Galyna
Andrushko, 22–23, James Thew, cover (bottom right), 1 (right), Jiang Hongyan (pinwheels), 28–29, Jochen Kost,
10–11, Kokhanchikov, 4–5, Login (sun pattern), 4, 5, majeczka, 14–15, Markovka (leaf pattern), 8, nadiya_sergey,
24–25, pashabo (recycled paper texture), cover and throughout, Praseodimio, 12–13, Serg64 (sky), 28–29, 30–31,
32, SergeyIT, 8–9, Songquan Deng, 2–3

Note to Parents, Teachers, and Librarians
This Earth Matters book uses full color photographs and a nonfiction format to introduce the concept of
earth science and is designed to be read aloud to a pre-reader or to be read independently by an early reader.
Photographs help listeners and early readers understand the text and concepts discussed. The book encourages
further learning by including the following sections: Glossary, Read More, Internet Sites, and Index. Early
readers may need assistance using these features.

Printed in the United States of America in North Mankato, Minnesota.
092012   006933CGS13